THIS BOOK BELONGS TO

_____

ORDER OF CONTENTS

HOME DETAILS

HOUSEHOLD BILLS

MAJOR APPLIANCES

KITCHEN

LIVING ROOM

DINING ROOM

MASTER BEDROOM

BEDROOM 2

BEDROOM 3

BEDROOM 4

BEDROOM 5

BATHROOM 1

BATHROOM 2

BATHROOM 3

BATHROOM 4

ENTRANCE / HALLWAY

GARDEN

CUSTOM ROOMS

HOME DETAILS

ADDRESS	
YEAR HOUSE WAS BUILT	
PURCHASE DATE	
PURCHASE PRICE	
MORTGAGE PROVIDER	
OTHER DETAILS	

HOUSEHOLD BILLS

		COST PER MONTH		
BILL	PROVIDER	YEAR 1	YEAR 2	YEAR 3

MAJOR APPLIANCES

	ON MOVING IN
BRAND	
SUPPLIED BY	
DATE PURCHASED	
COST	
MODEL / SERIAL	
WARRANTY	
DIMENSIONS	
	REPLACEMENT
BRAND	
SUPPLIED BY	
DATE PURCHASED	
COST	
MODEL / SERIAL	
WARRANTY	
DIMENSIONS	

MAJOR APPLIANCES

	ON MOVING IN
BRAND	
SUPPLIED BY	
DATE PURCHASED	
COST	
MODEL / SERIAL	
WARRANTY	
DIMENSIONS	
	REPLACEMENT
BRAND	
SUPPLIED BY	
DATE PURCHASED	
COST	
MODEL / SERIAL	
WARRANTY	
DIMENSIONS	

MAJOR APPLIANCES

	ON MOVING IN
BRAND	
SUPPLIED BY	
DATE PURCHASED	
COST	
MODEL / SERIAL	
WARRANTY	
DIMENSIONS	
	REPLACEMENT
BRAND	
SUPPLIED BY	
DATE PURCHASED	
COST	
MODEL / SERIAL	
WARRANTY	
DIMENSIONS	

MAJOR APPLIANCES

	ON MOVING IN
BRAND	
SUPPLIED BY	
DATE PURCHASED	
COST	
MODEL / SERIAL	
WARRANTY	
DIMENSIONS	
	REPLACEMENT
BRAND	
SUPPLIED BY	
DATE PURCHASED	
COST	
MODEL / SERIAL	
WARRANTY	
DIMENSIONS	

MAJOR APPLIANCES

	ON MOVING IN
BRAND	
SUPPLIED BY	
DATE PURCHASED	
COST	
MODEL / SERIAL	
WARRANTY	
DIMENSIONS	
	REPLACEMENT
BRAND	
SUPPLIED BY	
DATE PURCHASED	
COST	
MODEL / SERIAL	
WARRANTY	
DIMENSIONS	

MAJOR APPLIANCES

	ON MOVING IN
BRAND	
SUPPLIED BY	
DATE PURCHASED	
COST	
MODEL / SERIAL	
WARRANTY	
DIMENSIONS	
	REPLACEMENT
BRAND	
SUPPLIED BY	
DATE PURCHASED	
COST	
MODEL / SERIAL	
WARRANTY	
DIMENSIONS	

MAJOR APPLIANCES

	ON MOVING IN
BRAND	
SUPPLIED BY	
DATE PURCHASED	
COST	
MODEL / SERIAL	
WARRANTY	
DIMENSIONS	
	REPLACEMENT
BRAND	
SUPPLIED BY	
DATE PURCHASED	
COST	
MODEL / SERIAL	
WARRANTY	
DIMENSIONS	

INTERIOR DESIGN PLAN

KITCHEN

DIMENSIONS _____

OF WINDOWS _____   # OF DOORS _____

WINDOW 1 SIZE _____   DOOR 1 _____

WINDOW 2 SIZE _____   DOOR 2 _____

WINDOW 3 SIZE _____   DOOR 3 _____

COLOR / STYLE _____

    WALLS _____

    FLOOR _____

    CEILING _____

    TRIM _____

    DOORS _____

NOTES / IDEAS

KITCHEN LAYOUT PLAN

KITCHEN TO DO LIST

TASK	FINISHED

KITCHEN QUOTES

DATE	COMPANY	SERVICE/JOB	PRICE	THOUGHTS

PURCHASED KITCHEN ITEMS

ITEM	SUPPLIER	COST
	TOTAL	

NOTES

INTERIOR DESIGN PLAN

LIVING ROOM

DIMENSIONS _____

OF WINDOWS _____ # OF DOORS _____

WINDOW 1 SIZE _____ DOOR 1 _____

WINDOW 2 SIZE _____ DOOR 2 _____

WINDOW 3 SIZE _____ DOOR 3 _____

COLOR / STYLE _____

    WALLS _____

    FLOOR _____

    CEILING _____

    TRIM _____

    DOORS _____

NOTES / IDEAS

LIVING ROOM PLAN

LIVING ROOM TO DO LIST

TASK	FINISHED

LIVING ROOM QUOTES

DATE	COMPANY	SERVICE/JOB	PRICE	THOUGHTS

PURCHASED LIVING ROOM ITEMS

ITEM	SUPPLIER	COST
	TOTAL	

NOTES

INTERIOR DESIGN PLAN

DINING ROOM

DIMENSIONS _____

OF WINDOWS _____   # OF DOORS _____

WINDOW 1 SIZE _____   DOOR 1 _____

WINDOW 2 SIZE _____   DOOR 2 _____

WINDOW 3 SIZE _____   DOOR 3 _____

COLOR / STYLE _____

    WALLS _____

    FLOOR _____

    CEILING _____

    TRIM _____

    DOORS _____

NOTES / IDEAS

DINING ROOM PLAN

DINING ROOM TO DO LIST

TASK	FINISHED

DINING ROOM QUOTES

DATE	COMPANY	SERVICE/JOB	PRICE	THOUGHTS

PURCHASED DINING ROOM ITEMS

ITEM	SUPPLIER	COST
	TOTAL	

NOTES

INTERIOR DESIGN PLAN

MASTER BEDROOM

DIMENSIONS _____

# OF WINDOWS	_____	# OF DOORS	_____
WINDOW 1 SIZE	_____	DOOR 1	_____
WINDOW 2 SIZE	_____	DOOR 2	_____
WINDOW 3 SIZE	_____	DOOR 3	_____

COLOR / STYLE _____

- WALLS _____
- FLOOR _____
- CEILING _____
- TRIM _____
- DOORS _____

NOTES / IDEAS

MASTER BEDROOM PLAN

MASTER BEDROOM TO DO LIST

TASK	FINISHED

MASTER BEDROOM QUOTES

DATE	COMPANY	SERVICE/JOB	PRICE	THOUGHTS

PURCHASED MASTER BEDROOM ITEMS

ITEM	SUPPLIER	COST
	TOTAL	

NOTES

INTERIOR DESIGN PLAN

BEDROOM 2

DIMENSIONS _____

OF WINDOWS _____ # OF DOORS _____

WINDOW 1 SIZE _____ DOOR 1 _____

WINDOW 2 SIZE _____ DOOR 2 _____

WINDOW 3 SIZE _____ DOOR 3 _____

COLOR / STYLE _____

    WALLS _____

    FLOOR _____

    CEILING _____

    TRIM _____

    DOORS _____

NOTES / IDEAS

BEDROOM 2 PLAN

BEDROOM 2 TO DO LIST

TASK	FINISHED

BEDROOM 2 QUOTES

DATE	COMPANY	SERVICE/JOB	PRICE	THOUGHTS

PURCHASED BEDROOM 2 ITEMS

ITEM	SUPPLIER	COST
	TOTAL	

NOTES

INTERIOR DESIGN PLAN

BEDROOM 3

DIMENSIONS _____

OF WINDOWS _____ # OF DOORS _____

WINDOW 1 SIZE _____ DOOR 1 _____

WINDOW 2 SIZE _____ DOOR 2 _____

WINDOW 3 SIZE _____ DOOR 3 _____

COLOR / STYLE _____

    WALLS _____

    FLOOR _____

    CEILING _____

    TRIM _____

    DOORS _____

NOTES / IDEAS

BEDROOM 3 PLAN

BEDROOM 3 TO DO LIST

TASK	FINISHED

BEDROOM 3 QUOTES

DATE	COMPANY	SERVICE/JOB	PRICE	THOUGHTS

PURCHASED BEDROOM 3 ITEMS

ITEM	SUPPLIER	COST
	TOTAL	

NOTES

INTERIOR DESIGN PLAN

BEDROOM 4

DIMENSIONS   _____

OF WINDOWS   _____   # OF DOORS   _____

WINDOW 1 SIZE   _____   DOOR 1   _____

WINDOW 2 SIZE   _____   DOOR 2   _____

WINDOW 3 SIZE   _____   DOOR 3   _____

COLOR / STYLE   _____

    WALLS   _____

    FLOOR   _____

    CEILING   _____

    TRIM   _____

    DOORS   _____

NOTES / IDEAS

BEDROOM 4 PLAN

BEDROOM 4 TO DO LIST

TASK	FINISHED

BEDROOM 4 QUOTES

DATE	COMPANY	SERVICE/JOB	PRICE	THOUGHTS

PURCHASED BEDROOM 4 ITEMS

ITEM	SUPPLIER	COST
	TOTAL	

NOTES

INTERIOR DESIGN PLAN

BEDROOM 5

DIMENSIONS _____

OF WINDOWS _____   # OF DOORS _____

WINDOW 1 SIZE _____   DOOR 1 _____

WINDOW 2 SIZE _____   DOOR 2 _____

WINDOW 3 SIZE _____   DOOR 3 _____

COLOR / STYLE _____

    WALLS _____

    FLOOR _____

    CEILING _____

    TRIM _____

    DOORS _____

NOTES / IDEAS

BEDROOM 5 PLAN

BEDROOM 5 TO DO LIST

TASK	FINISHED

BEDROOM 5 QUOTES

DATE	COMPANY	SERVICE/JOB	PRICE	THOUGHTS

PURCHASED BEDROOM 5 ITEMS

ITEM	SUPPLIER	COST
	TOTAL	

NOTES

INTERIOR DESIGN PLAN

BATHROOM 1

DIMENSIONS _____

OF WINDOWS _____ # OF DOORS _____

WINDOW 1 SIZE _____ DOOR 1 _____

WINDOW 2 SIZE _____ DOOR 2 _____

WINDOW 3 SIZE _____ DOOR 3 _____

COLOR / STYLE _____

    WALLS _____

    FLOOR _____

    CEILING _____

    TRIM _____

    DOORS _____

NOTES / IDEAS

BATHROOM PLAN

BATHROOM 1 TO DO LIST

TASK	FINISHED

BATHROOM I QUOTES

DATE	COMPANY	SERVICE/JOB	PRICE	THOUGHTS

PURCHASED BATHROOM ITEMS

ITEM	SUPPLIER	COST
	TOTAL	

NOTES

INTERIOR DESIGN PLAN

BATHROOM 2

DIMENSIONS _____

OF WINDOWS _____ # OF DOORS _____

WINDOW 1 SIZE _____ DOOR 1 _____

WINDOW 2 SIZE _____ DOOR 2 _____

WINDOW 3 SIZE _____ DOOR 3 _____

COLOR / STYLE _____

    WALLS _____

    FLOOR _____

    CEILING _____

    TRIM _____

    DOORS _____

<u>NOTES / IDEAS</u>

BATHROOM 2 PLAN

BATHROOM 2 TO DO LIST

TASK	FINISHED

BATHROOM 2 QUOTES

DATE	COMPANY	SERVICE/JOB	PRICE	THOUGHTS

PURCHASED BATHROOM 2 ITEMS

ITEM	SUPPLIER	COST
	TOTAL	

NOTES

INTERIOR DESIGN PLAN

BATHROOM 3

DIMENSIONS _____

OF WINDOWS _____   # OF DOORS _____

WINDOW 1 SIZE _____   DOOR 1 _____

WINDOW 2 SIZE _____   DOOR 2 _____

WINDOW 3 SIZE _____   DOOR 3 _____

COLOR / STYLE _____

   WALLS _____

   FLOOR _____

   CEILING _____

   TRIM _____

   DOORS _____

<u>NOTES / IDEAS</u>

BATHROOM 3 PLAN

BATHROOM 3 TO DO LIST

TASK	FINISHED

BATHROOM 3 QUOTES

DATE	COMPANY	SERVICE/JOB	PRICE	THOUGHTS

PURCHASED BATHROOM 3 ITEMS

ITEM	SUPPLIER	COST
	TOTAL	

NOTES

INTERIOR DESIGN PLAN

BATHROOM 4

DIMENSIONS _____

OF WINDOWS _____ # OF DOORS _____

WINDOW 1 SIZE _____ DOOR 1 _____

WINDOW 2 SIZE _____ DOOR 2 _____

WINDOW 3 SIZE _____ DOOR 3 _____

COLOR / STYLE _____

    WALLS _____

    FLOOR _____

    CEILING _____

    TRIM _____

    DOORS _____

NOTES / IDEAS

BATHROOM 4 PLAN

BATHROOM 4 TO DO LIST

TASK	FINISHED

BATHROOM 4 QUOTES

DATE	COMPANY	SERVICE/JOB	PRICE	THOUGHTS

PURCHASED BATHROOM 4 ITEMS

ITEM	SUPPLIER	COST
	TOTAL	

NOTES

INTERIOR DESIGN PLAN

ENTRANCE / HALLWAY

DIMENSIONS _____

OF WINDOWS _____ # OF DOORS _____

WINDOW 1 SIZE _____ DOOR 1 _____

WINDOW 2 SIZE _____ DOOR 2 _____

WINDOW 3 SIZE _____ DOOR 3 _____

COLOR / STYLE _____

    WALLS _____

    FLOOR _____

    CEILING _____

    TRIM _____

    DOORS _____

NOTES / IDEAS

ENTRANCE / HALLWAY PLAN

ENTRANCE / HALLWAY TO DO LIST

TASK	FINISHED

ENTRANCE / HALLWAY QUOTES

DATE	COMPANY	SERVICE/JOB	PRICE	THOUGHTS

PURCHASED ENTRANCE / HALLWAY ITEMS

ITEM	SUPPLIER	COST
	TOTAL	

NOTES

DESIGN PLAN

GARDEN

DIMENSIONS _____

_____   _____

_____   _____

_____   _____

_____   _____

COLOR / STYLE _____

FENCE _____

GROUND _____

LIGHTING _____

SEATING _____

DECKING _____

NOTES / IDEAS

GARDEN PLAN

GARDEN TO DO LIST

TASK	FINISHED

GARDEN QUOTES

DATE	COMPANY	SERVICE/JOB	PRICE	THOUGHTS

PURCHASED GARDEN ITEMS

ITEM	SUPPLIER	COST
	TOTAL	

NOTES

INTERIOR DESIGN PLAN

_____

DIMENSIONS _____

OF WINDOWS _____   # OF DOORS _____

WINDOW 1 SIZE _____   DOOR 1 _____

WINDOW 2 SIZE _____   DOOR 2 _____

WINDOW 3 SIZE _____   DOOR 3 _____

COLOR / STYLE _____

WALLS _____

FLOOR _____

CEILING _____

TRIM _____

DOORS _____

NOTES / IDEAS

_____ PLAN

_____ TO DO LIST

TASK	FINISHED

_____ QUOTES

DATE	COMPANY	SERVICE/JOB	PRICE	THOUGHTS

PURCHASED _____ ITEMS

ITEM	SUPPLIER	COST
	TOTAL	

NOTES

INTERIOR DESIGN PLAN

_____

DIMENSIONS _____

OF WINDOWS _____ # OF DOORS _____

WINDOW 1 SIZE _____ DOOR 1 _____

WINDOW 2 SIZE _____ DOOR 2 _____

WINDOW 3 SIZE _____ DOOR 3 _____

COLOR / STYLE _____

    WALLS _____

    FLOOR _____

    CEILING _____

    TRIM _____

    DOORS _____

NOTES / IDEAS

_____ PLAN

_____ TO DO LIST

TASK	FINISHED

_____ QUOTES

DATE	COMPANY	SERVICE/JOB	PRICE	THOUGHTS

PURCHASED _____ ITEMS

ITEM	SUPPLIER	COST
	TOTAL	

NOTES

INTERIOR DESIGN PLAN

_____

DIMENSIONS   _____

OF WINDOWS   _____   # OF DOORS   _____

WINDOW 1 SIZE   _____   DOOR 1   _____

WINDOW 2 SIZE   _____   DOOR 2   _____

WINDOW 3 SIZE   _____   DOOR 3   _____

COLOR / STYLE   _____

    WALLS   _____

    FLOOR   _____

    CEILING   _____

    TRIM   _____

    DOORS   _____

<u>NOTES / IDEAS</u>

_____ PLAN

_____ TO DO LIST

TASK	FINISHED

_____ QUOTES

DATE	COMPANY	SERVICE/JOB	PRICE	THOUGHTS

PURCHASED _____ ITEMS

ITEM	SUPPLIER	COST
	TOTAL	

NOTES

INTERIOR DESIGN PLAN

_____

DIMENSIONS _____

OF WINDOWS _____ # OF DOORS _____

WINDOW 1 SIZE _____ DOOR 1 _____

WINDOW 2 SIZE _____ DOOR 2 _____

WINDOW 3 SIZE _____ DOOR 3 _____

COLOR / STYLE _____

    WALLS _____

    FLOOR _____

    CEILING _____

    TRIM _____

    DOORS _____

NOTES / IDEAS

_____ PLAN

_____ TO DO LIST

TASK	FINISHED

_____ QUOTES

DATE	COMPANY	SERVICE/JOB	PRICE	THOUGHTS

PURCHASED _____ ITEMS

ITEM	SUPPLIER	COST
	TOTAL	

NOTES

NOTES

Printed in Great Britain
by Amazon